Leadership

: Techniques and Methods of Proven Leadership That Will Help You Discover the Real Leader That Lies Within You

(Leadership that Inspires Others and Leadership Taking Command of Leadership)

Mitch Phelps

TABLE OF CONTENT

Introduction

We would like to take this opportunity to welcome you to Leadership: Influential Leadership Skills for Mastering Business Communication, Management Conversations, and Team Building. This all-encompassing book eliminates the fluff in order to give useful knowledge that you can begin putting to use right away. For example, rather than spending page after page discussing the chemical processes that take place inside our brains when we speak, or using jargon that is decades old and taken from outdated textbooks, the authors of this book cut out the filler. Each page has pertinent material that is ready to be used, and the reader is actively urged to contribute to the knowledge that is provided and make use of it to establish their own particular methods and style. The book was written to be read from beginning to end; but, if a certain chapter is of special interest to you, please feel free to hop forward to it. For example, if you are interested in getting a pay raise today, you may want to skip ahead to the section titled "Influential Phrases."

Each part provides an in-depth examination of a distinct subject. They are ordered in such a way as to build upon each other as they go towards the final chapter, which will explain how to put everything together as well as which forms of leadership and ways of communication are most effective in a given circumstance.

You will have a better understanding of what your superiors and team members expect from you as a leader as a result of the high-level content that is presented throughout this book. You will also learn how to manage and direct these expectations so that they consistently lead to favorable results. This book contains a variety of models, strategies, and tactics that cover a wide range of themes and issues. These models, strategies, and tactics may be used alone or in combination to express your views and direct interactions with any number of different individuals in any given circumstance. This book is primarily framed within the context of the workplace; however, whether you are a football coach, sales manager, financial advisor, or entrepreneur, this book contains information relevant to your day-to-day business interactions, and when utilized appropriately, it will significantly improve both your output and your ability to advance within your chosen field.

This book is centered on your experiences and should be combined with the information that you currently possess in order to achieve the goal of having a stronger impact within both your workplace and the industry as a whole. If you go through the exercises and use the models provided for making decisions, you will discover that you have increased confidence in both your ability to manage and to delegate tasks.

Understand and discover how to coach people to achieve their best achievements via the use of Systematic Thinking, comprehension, and feedback, all while boosting the functioning and productivity of any team using the proven approaches for outcome management that are discussed in Managing Outcomes.

The chapters "Influential Phrases You can use Today" and "Quick Fire Tactics You can use Today" were written with the intention of providing, at a glance, helpful advice and strategies on the most efficient methods to ask inquiries, make requests, and delegate tasks.

Your crew is the most valuable resource at your disposal. Their one-of-a-kind set of abilities and beliefs will contribute to the results of the group in ways that will often seem to be random. However, if you work on developing both yourself and your team, you will start to see patterns within the system, have a better feel of what will happen next, and be aware of the appropriate communication and management styles to use in order to effectively impact the situation and bring about the end you want. Do not allow yourself to be controlled by your environment; instead, cultivate, improve, and perfect your abilities to communicate, exert influence, and make decisions in order to become the most powerful leader you possibly can.

What Is Leadership?

Having strong leadership abilities is one of the most important factors that contribute to success. The fact that some of the most successful individuals in the world also have strong leadership abilities is the primary reason why they are able to accomplish what they set out to do in the first place. Good leaders are not always born, despite the widespread misconception to the contrary. Leadership abilities are truly something that can be honed and developed over the course of time and experience.

You will learn in this chapter what leadership is, the many forms of leadership, and what societal expectations are placed on a leader. Additionally, it enables you to differentiate the concept of "leadership" from other phrases that are relatively similar, such as "management" and "coaching."

People have varying perspectives on what leadership entails, but there is one definition of leadership that is universally accepted: leadership is the capacity of an individual to guide the actions of a group of people, an organization, or both. Strong leaders are able to direct people in the execution of predetermined plans of action. Effective leaders are able to inspire the members of a group to do the duties that have been assigned to them. As a leader of a group, your primary responsibility is to facilitate everyone's progress toward the overarching objective of the organization.

It would be helpful for you to have a better understanding of leadership if you were more aware with the many forms that it may take. The following are examples of some of the styles of leadership that are now in widespread use:

The Leadership Style of Laissez-Faire

Because it does not need the leader to actively monitor the members of his group, this type of leadership is not the most effective kind of leadership. Laissez-faire leadership, which is often referred to as delegative leadership, is a style of leadership in which the leader abdicates decision-making authority to the members of the group. This type of leadership is defined by limited direction and supervision from the leader, easy access to resources and tools required by the members of the group in order for them to make their own choices, members of the group who are expected to discover answers to issues on their own, and the handing up of authority to followers.

Nevertheless, the leaders who employ this style of leadership accept responsibility for whatever choice or action the group makes. Because the leader does not actively monitor his followers under this model, it has the lowest rate of production out of all the other leadership styles.

Leadership based on absolute power

This type of leadership has the advantage of allowing the leader to make choices autonomously, which is a significant benefit. He is able to successfully impose his will on other individuals and has total control over the processes involved in decision-making. On the other hand, one of the drawbacks of adopting such a style of leadership is that it restricts the amount of personal liberty enjoyed by the members of the organization. They have no choice but to do what their boss instructs them. There are also situations in which the members are prevented from asking inquiries or expressing their grievances.

Leadership based on participant input

This is a model of leadership that is up there with the best there is. Simply said, the leader encourages participation from the members of the group in the many activities, initiatives, and programs that have been planned. He makes certain that everyone has something of value to contribute to their imminent success. He invites participation from his members in the different decision-making processes that are available. Take note, however, that the leader is ultimately responsible for making the choice.

The fantastic thing about participatory leadership is that the leader is prepared to examine the ideas of his followers and figure out which among the solutions offered by his members might work to the benefit of the complete team. The other amazing thing about participative leadership is that it encourages followers to take an active role in decision-making. This has the potential to make the members feel more involved, which will make it simpler to motivate them to work together.

Leadership based on transactions

This style of leadership places an emphasis on the financial side of being a leader. It aims to reward excellent achievements and punish poor ones in order to achieve its goals. The leader establishes goals and monitors the progress of his followers as they carry out the many responsibilities that have been given to them individually. At the conclusion of it all, the leader will analyze their performances and choose the prizes and punishments that are most appropriate for each individual.

Leadership that enables transformational change

If you are able to create clear lines of communication, you may anticipate that this type of leadership will be successful. The primary objective of the leader is to motivate, inspire, and convince the members of his group to carry out a certain activity without resorting to coercion or other coercive methods. The members of the group benefit greatly from this form of leadership since it enables them to grow into better versions of themselves.

Mode of Leadership Based on Coaching

This style of leadership is defined by leaders that clearly identify the responsibilities and duties that each of their followers are expected to carry out and play. This kind of leadership is also known as servant leadership. In addition, they look to their followers for recommendations and other forms of feedback. The coaching leadership style maintains a two-way type of communication, despite the fact that the leader retains ultimate decision-making authority over the organization.

It is reasonable to anticipate that coaching leaders will operate more successfully in environments in which improvements in terms of outcomes and performance are required. When it comes to assisting others in developing their talents and advancing their careers, good coaching leaders are very successful. They assist their colleagues in developing their core competencies and provide direction whenever it is required.

They are also capable of encouraging, motivating, and inspiring their members, and they are able to establish a more favorable atmosphere in the workplace. The coaching method of leadership is most successful when used to individuals who are more amenable, experienced, and responsible.

Strategies For Efficient Leadership Of Groups And Teams

One of those tasks that, on the surface, seems to be straightforward is leading a group of people. In actual use, it may turn out to be a very challenging job. In order to become an effective leader of a group, what specific strategies should you implement?

Create a Persuasive Argument Vision that is both imaginative and prescient

To be a successful leader, you need followers. If you want other people to follow you, you need to be able to create a clear picture of what the future will probably be like and why they need to be a part of building this wonderful future. If you don't do this, your hearts and ideas will never engage with one another.

Accept Yourself as You Are

Because you are a human, you will have some powers at your disposal. These may take the form of skill, experience, or insight; they might also take the form of particular attributes. Concurrently, it's possible that you have other places that aren't as powerful. If you have these insights, you will not only have a better grasp of the situation, but you will also be able to better direct where you focus your time and effort and figure out the composition of your own team as a result.

Learn more about the members of your team.

I'm usually shocked by how much work we make into finding out about the shortcomings and strengths of new recruits, such as the fact that we only spend a fraction of that time studying our current personnel. I'm always startled by how much attention we put into finding out about the weaknesses and strengths of new hires. Having a good understanding of your team allows for more accurate job and responsibility assignment. It is also likely that this may aid with motivation, since it will make it easier to assign tasks that excites them.

Set Aside Specific Objectives

Goals that are too vague will lead to outcomes that are sub-optimal at best, and non-existent at worst. To achieve your objectives, you should be as detailed as you possibly can. Focus on guiding them to action-oriented and hang time restrictions as your primary objective. You may, if you like, separate them into more manageable milestones along the way.

Put your focus on establishing trust.

If a team does not have adequate faith in its ability, it might end up failing. There are instances when it is simple do things that increases trust, such as living up to one's promises or treating everyone the same.

Keep people accountable at all times.

The fact that the leader continually lets individuals off the hook is perhaps the part about the team that is the most discouraging. Obviously, there will be times when there are legitimate primary reasons why someone cannot achieve what they promised. Concurrently, there may be those who consistently under-deliver on what they promise, just due to the fact that they are aware that there would be no follow-through.

Employ Your Mouth and Ears in the Appropriate Ratio in Order to Succeed

To put it another way, you and the other members of your team need to work on improving your ability to pay attention to one another. My impression is that individuals struggle the most when it comes to the skill of listening. Bear in mind that you only have one mouth while having two ears.

The conclusion is that achieving success as a leader is not guaranteed; nonetheless, there are a few basic elements that may have a significant impact on your level of success as a leader of a group.

Leadership That Exudes Charisma

Leaders that use this type of leadership are naturally persuasive and are able to utilize their charm and attractive personality to guarantee that their organization is successful in whatever endeavors they undertake. They are firm in their beliefs and give their all to the cause they support. It's true that transformational leaders and charismatic leaders have a few things in common, but in terms of audience and emphasis, these two types of leaders couldn't be more different. While the former are concerned with enhancing the current situation, the later are concerned with transforming the group in accordance with the vision of the leader.

Comparison between Leadership and Coaching

The terms "leadership" and "coaching" are often used interchangeably in modern parlance. These two words are not interchangeable, despite the fact that they have certain similarities. You will learn the why and the how in the next section.

One of the key distinctions between leadership and coaching is that the former is more of a lifestyle choice, while the latter is more of an element of your life as a whole. There is a strict prohibition on engaging in such behavior while on the job. You may be a leader even if you are not one in the organization in which you work. For instance, you may guide the members of your family to do certain tasks at home in a more effective manner.

On the other hand, coaching is more of a process than anything else. It's possible for leaders to pursue things via the coaching process. If you are in a position of leadership, then it is your responsibility to guarantee that the members of your group will carry out the responsibilities that they have been given and will obey the commands that you give them. On the other hand, coaching is more targeted in the sense that it must tackle a particular challenge or issue that calls for their aid in order to be successful.

When compared to leadership, coaching often only lasts for a limited amount of time. It lays forth objectives that must be accomplished within a certain amount of time. The coaching profession often requires skills that are technical in nature. The following are some other characteristics that differentiate a leader from a coach in contrast to one another:

Talking to people and providing them with instructions takes up a significant portion of a leader's time. On the other side, a coach should spend the majority of their time asking questions and listening to the team they are coaching.

It is necessary for a leader to draw hasty inferences based on the information that is provided to him. A coach, on the other hand, must first spend time watching before forming any kind of presumption about the players under their tutelage.

When searching for answers to issues, a leader would often go for the most direct and efficient path. On the other hand, in order to get to the bottom of a problem, a coach has to dig deeper and unearth any underlying difficulties.

Strong Moral and Ethical Foundations

Some people refer to them as spiritual laws, spiritual standards, or spiritual truths; I, on the other hand, sometimes refer to them as spiritual systems. They represent a component of the approach that we take to life. These are ways of being, doing, pondering, thinking, continuing on, and engaging with life that have the potential to enable us to live up to our most significant potential. In a sense, you might say that these are the rules of the game. In addition to this, they do not adhere to any one "religious" doctrine.

The majority of people spend their lives virtually thoughtlessly, and the majority of the time they do it on autopilot. The more cautious we are able to become, and the more aware of these greater truths we are as we collaborate with the universe, the less suffering we will experience, the more progress we will make, and the more meaning and satisfaction we will uncover in this life. In this part of the discussion, we're going to take a look at some of the most significant spiritual precepts and investigate how we may apply them in our day-to-day lives.

Expressing gratitude. The stability provided by routine is a gift, as is each and every breath. In this life, there is nothing that can be taken lightly. The realization that one has reasons to be grateful, generally, generally, and especially, seems to eliminate a considerable portion of the frivolous and typical irritability that so many of us experience. To be more precise, it seems to prevent feelings of annoyance, fretfulness, scorn, wrath, and resentment from occurring. When you first open your eyes in the morning, when you close them before going to sleep, and when you wake up in the middle of the day, there is something extremely invigorating about filling yourself with a sense of thankfulness. thankfulness for all that you've allowed to happen to you, as well as thankfulness for everything that hasn't happened to you.

Behave with humility and modesty. It's possible that modesty is one of the aspects of the human experience that gets misinterpreted and underestimated the most. This does not imply lowering yourself behind other people, allowing other people to abuse you, or behaving as if you are mediocre or worthless in any form. Simply said, it means not favoring someone over another and letting go of the impulse to elevate oneself above others. Unquestionably, an excessive amount of human energy is lost in the thoughtless pursuit of criticality, getting one-up, and seeking to show that we are richer, better, more astute, smarter, sharper, more capable, or more admirable than others. There is no need for you to engage in amusements with other people that are based on a feeling of self-rivalry or status. The recovery of your creative energy and the opening up of extra space for its use in the course of your growth are both wonderful benefits of solitude. When we let go of the need to believe that we are better than other people, we give ourselves the opportunity to develop and succeed.

Keeping a cheerful attitude and an optimistic outlook no matter what the circumstances. I'll save you the clichéd cliches about glasses that are half-full and half-empty because I'm going to explain something to you. Many people think of confidence not as only a childlike faith or certainty that something wonderful will occur, but rather as an active state of mind that can be achieved through effort. It is in the nature of many people to behave in such a way as to pave the way for extraordinary things to take place. A better maxim would be "Things turn out generally advantageous in the event that you make the best of the way things turn out." It's the certainty that a major portion of the inferences we want are, without a shadow of a doubt, within our reach. We are not able to control all of the possibilities; yet, as humans, we are purposefully minded creatures, and we adapt our actions to the reality as it presents itself to us.

In the same vein, it doesn't care about the slogans that promote "positive thinking." It's all about making productive choices. This particular interpretation of idealism forms the very core of creativity, progress, innovation, and the process of reinvention. Inquisitively, idealism is also a way for benefitting from luckiness. The pioneering doctor and expert Louis Pasteur once observed, "Chance supports the arranged personality." The more optimistic we are, the better our chances are of acquiring the resources we need to maintain ourselves.

Being Generous to One Another in Giving. Getting people out of their narcissistic conscience bubbles and encouraging them to do pleasant things for other people is one of the finest antitoxins for the grumpiness, aggravation, scorn, loss of reason, and self-centeredness that harrow such a variety of folks in their later years. This is one of the reasons why helping others is one of the most important antitoxins. Many experts in the area of anxiety say that if you want to be happy and fulfilled, you should try to conduct your life in such a way that you earn the praise of your friends and family. When someone has a long-standing perception that they are the victim, the one who is taken advantage of, or the one who always gets taken advantage of, it may make them feel diminished, guarded, and walled in.

The simple act of providing for other people makes us feel more powerful, whole, fascinated, and captivating. It also makes us feel larger, stronger, and fuller. Giving your spare change to a homeless person; giving someone the right of way in traffic when you don't have to; saying something nice to a server or store representative who seems a bit exhausted and not getting a charge out of life; doing little supports without being asked; welcoming your depressed neighbor, regardless of the fact that he doesn't welcome you back; demonstrating to others that you think about them; saying please and thank you. These are all examples of acts of kindness. Giving helps us grow as individuals.

This Is My Great Opportunity

My chance presented itself when it was observed by my employer how hard I had been working. I was asked to fill in as the quality assurance manager at a factory when that position became vacant. I didn't know what to do with the little plant since I couldn't see it well enough. I was set up in a motel in a valley in rural California, in a little town, adjacent to a motorcycle bar. The hotel was provided for me. They would continue to party into the wee hours of the morning, and I would sometimes wake up to the sound of what I could only imagine were enormous, hairy guys stomping about outside my door. I put a chair in front of the doorknob and crossed my fingers that no one would try to kick it in. During the first month, I had a hard time falling or staying asleep.

I would get out of bed and drive to the factory in the morning, where I would then go to the staff meeting while making an effort to keep my head down. The manager of the factory would ask for information that I did not have and was unsure how to get. There were a few of uncomfortable exchanges that took place, and I am certain that he desired for me to be returned to the corporate lab as soon as possible. Things weren't looking good at all.

THE MENTORING THAT SERVED AS AN INSPIRATION

To my good fortune, I had a guide come into my life at that very moment. My possibilities for professional growth within the firm would have been severely limited if it were not for the fact that he served as the regional quality assurance manager for the organization.

He instructed me on how to be an effective manager, how to research problems, how to communicate with clients, and how to distribute responsibilities to my staff.

After everything started going in the right direction, the plant manager expressed his gratitude to having me on the team. When he asked me whether I wanted to continue working there permanently, that was the moment when everything shifted for me. Since I could not leave Colorado with my fiancée at the time since she was still there, I respectfully refused the offer and returned to Denver instead.

My immediate supervisor was the recipient of a letter of gratitude from the plant manager, which she promptly sent to me with the simple remark, "Good Job." My supervisor had incredibly high expectations, and I just sometimes heard a complement from her. It was a moment that I will always remember as being really proud of my profession. That letter is still in my possession.

The moral of the tale is that you do not have to face challenges by yourself and have faith that everything will turn out well in the end. You are not required to put on an act or make an attempt to find it out on your own.

The act of coaching

When is the use of coaching absolutely necessary? How do you determine when it is appropriate to coach? Coaching is aimed to bring about changes in behavior. Think of changes in behavior as modifiable risk factors for a patient who has heart disease. These are qualities of the person that are within the patient's control and may be altered.

When certain conditions are met within a company, it may become essential to implement coaching. The majority of the time, an individual's management will coach them in order to help them improve their performance and their skill set. This is a kind of coaching that places an emphasis on fundamental abilities that must be had in order to properly carry out job obligations and complete assigned tasks. The goal of skills coaching is to improve an individual's fundamental abilities so that they can contribute more to the general well-being and expansion of the organization or institution.

The following are some other examples of possible scenarios:

Coaching for change management is often carried out in advance of significant changes in an organization's organizational structure or pattern of work. This assists in aligning the individual's attitude and behavior with the new work structure and conditions to maximize production. Everyone involved would benefit from this as it would make it easier to acclimate to the new adjustments and cognitively comprehend the changes.

Consider a time in the past when you were concerned about changes in the leadership of an organization, such as a manager. Your staff will experience the same worry or fear as everyone else. Think of the upcoming transition as a chance for personal development, and communicate this to the team. This presents you with a chance to lead through any disruptions to the procedures you normally follow.

The individual's professional interests are the primary focal point of career counseling sessions. The individual's professional skills are evaluated, and the coach works with the client to assist him make adjustments and enhance his work performance. It results in a personal reevaluation of one's professional perspective and growth plan, with the end result being that the person being coached emerges with a greater clarity in regard to their career awareness. The employee is better able to adjust to the shift in his or her assigned job or work position within the business as a result of this counseling.

People who are receiving counseling on a very intimate level are the primary focus of personal life coaching. It investigates their goals, requirements, and desires, as well as everything they need to get out of life and everything they want to get out of themselves. They are given the assistance they need to make adjustments that will reposition them in life via the process of personal or life coaching.

The objective of coaching for improving team facilitation within an organization is to increase production toward the achievement of a certain goal. Team facilitation has a significant impact on an individual's level of self-confidence as well as the performance of a team when it comes to the formulation of strategies and the completion of tasks.

If we were in a clinical environment, this would be referred to as giving the care team strategic guidance. For instance, thirty percent of those diagnosed with diabetes do not have enough control over their condition. The new emphasis is on improving the population's ability to keep their glucose levels under control. The coaching would entail having conversations with the team about how to get the disease management of diabetes under control.

It would be cheaper and more cost-effective for an organization to coach the present team if it were faced with a scarcity of abilities. This scenario occurs when an organization faces the challenge of not having enough team members to fill particular roles. They would be able to improve their talents via this intervention, which would make them qualified for any employment that could become available.

Let's concentrate on the principles of coaching now that you have determined when it is appropriate to coach.

In the culture of the modern workplace, coaching has established itself as the most successful method of employee engagement. Individuals are led to uncover insights, take responsibility, and establish actionable objectives on performance and growth via a process called coaching. Coaching is a continuous, interactive activity. Change that is sustainable is achieved via engagement with newly gained knowledge. The person in question does not have a defect or a lower intellect level. People have a tendency to get preoccupied with the issue at hand, to the point that they miss the point of the lesson.

Coaching is intended to serve as a tool for gleaning knowledge from one's previous experiences and fostering self-discovery in order to influence one's future results. It is essential for a leader to have a solid understanding of the circumstances in which coaching would not be productive. According to the HBR Guide to Coaching Employees (2015), issues with mental illness, breaches of legal policy (harassment), changes in the dynamics of the family, and states of emergency should be entrusted to specialists and discussed with a representative of the human resources department. It is also very important to avoid turning a coaching session become a complaining or pointing the finger session.

My three business partners all agreed, but a significant query lingered in the background: "Who would that be?"

I pointed out to them that one of the things that I had seen was that one of the most expensive aspects of our company was the printed packaging components. The provider of our packaging, which included cartons, labels, printed leaflets and brochures, was the business with whom we engaged in the greatest level of financial activity among all of our suppliers. We had a fruitful working relationship with that vendor, and I had developed a strong working connection with the CEO over the course of the previous year. When we had our most recent encounter, he mentioned to me that they were investigating a variety of options for growing their company in some manner.

"What if I seek a meeting with him next week on my vacation, just the two of us, so that he won't feel like he's being placed into an unpleasant situation with one of his key customers? Just think, if he's receptive to the proposal, we have another potential to boost margins further by making the purchase of our packaging requirements inside via our business partner rather than outside. Just think about it. It was decided by everyone there that I would be the one to organize the one-on-one meeting.

The conversation with the CEO of our supplier went quite well. On the whole scope of the strategy for the company acquisition, we were able to arrive at a consensus. He even made the observation that our alliance would enhance the cost foundation of our company to the point that we could reinvest the savings in advertising and business expansion. In addition, he said that the commercial team that is part of his company might be leveraged to take on the responsibility of expanding the volume of the site to an extent that is more than our forecasts for years two and three in our business plan.

We spent the day talking about and putting our strategy into actionable steps. He inquired as to whether or not it would be OK for him to include the head of the business development team in our discussion. I would only do it on the condition that I could count on the secrecy of his assurances. He smiled and then told me that he wanted to ask the same question of me since he didn't want to put his relationship with the corporation in jeopardy. After all, he was the one who provided the company's locations in the US with the necessary packing materials.

At the conclusion of the 10-hour day, we reached an agreement with a handshake and decided that he would charge his general counsel with drafting the official terms of the partnership, ownership, and financing needs. We agreed that he would delegate this responsibility. Despite the fact that we were running out of time and I was convinced they would agree with the agreement I'd struck, making the choice to go forward without the team's buy-in caused me some anxiety. However, I went ahead and made the decision anyway.

As soon as I checked into the hotel, I immediately contacted the other three members of the team, unable to contain my excitement. Thankfully, they shared my enthusiasm for the game. We were on the verge of purchasing our site and expanding the company when something unexpected happened.

The week after I returned from vacation, I was getting close to reaching another milestone. In order to present our business case and our offer for the site, we needed to schedule a meeting with the corporate project manager as soon as possible. It was imperative that we schedule and organize this meeting in advance of announcing the top three candidates for potential purchasers. My request for the call with the project manager, who was headquartered in the UK, was put under the general subject of "questions regarding the Aiken site sale process." The project manager was in the United Kingdom.

During this time period, email was still in its infancy, and we lacked the line speeds as well as the ability to electronically transfer huge files with one another. Therefore, making verbal presentations over the phone with the pledge to follow up with documentation utilizing intra-company mail was not unheard of and did not constitute a first. Finally, the time for the call came, and I was both apprehensive and enthusiastic about putting in a bid for the acquisition of the site. I felt like we were throwing our hat into the ring for it. I was certain that we had a sound business case that would be to the company's and our own financial advantage if we decided to go forward with it. We had reached an agreement to disclose some of our financial information, but not our intentions to increase our margins any more than what we were already proposing in exchange for the opportunity to cut our supplier prices by a large amount. In a nutshell, we had no intention of disclosing our successful method in order to allow others to implement it independently of us.

I began by expressing gratitude to the project manager for his time, and then I proceeded to immediately begin explaining the work that my team and I had done in order to present the firm with an offer to acquire the site from them. The answer I got from the project manager was certainly in the top five of "not what I expected!" events in my life and work, but there have been other instances in which my picture of how another person would respond to a proposal or circumstance missed the mark.

It wasn't simply that he was disinterested in what we had to offer. He was irascible in his rage. He accused me and the team of weakening the whole project by not completely committing ourselves in a successful sale and, subsequently, the transition to a new owner. He said this was because we did not work together. He then proceeded to imply, in a menacing tone, that I had ruined any possibility of being kept by the firm in another capacity, and that my chances of being retained by the potential owners had been put in jeopardy as a result.

So, let's start with the most critical partnerships for the CFO function.

The connection with the creditor is the most important one right now. They have to have faith in our chief financial officer. The ties we have with our professional advisers in the areas of accounting and taxes are also quite important to us. It is imperative that Allie has a strong connection with the partner in our accounting business. She is required to interact directly with members of the IRS and other regulatory agencies on occasion. She doesn't necessarily need to have a close connection with them, but she does need to know how to interact with them appropriately. Workers employed by the government belong to a separate species.

Tom said that it seems as if Allison is someone who is able to get along well with others. In addition, I have a sneaking suspicion that she is able to exploit some of these connections to compensate for her lack of knowledge in some fields, such as income taxation.

Ryan affirmed it to be the case. So long as you are aware of the things you do not know!

Excellent point. Tom brought his coffee cup up to his nose and inhaled the scent as he did so. He took a few sips of the coffee. What are your thoughts on the coffee prepared with a French press? he inquired of Ryan.

It's excellent. Ryan let out a giggle. But I won't be taking a whiff of it.

Perhaps the effort spent on perfecting coffee isn't worth it, but you have to admit that people are, don't you?

Certainly, Mr. Tom. The comparison can only be taken so far!

Tom concluded that after a cursory examination of Allison, his gut tells him that she is someone worth keeping.

In response, Ryan said, "I concur." I believe that Allie have the ability to pick up any skill or piece of information that may be necessary in order to go deeper into the position. She is having a little bit of difficulty right now, but as her experience grows, she will get better and better.

It would seem that the foremost objective at this point is to secure her safety by whatever means necessary. Do you have any more recent conversations with her? Tom had inquired.

She expressed her regret for her overreaction in a very lengthy email that she had written to me. I believe that we will retain her, but there is no question that we will need to make some adjustments. For example, finding her some skilled additional assistance to lighten the load.

After going through the capabilities with Allison, what are some things that come to mind when you think of Ed?

On the bright side, Ed is well-versed in the industry and maintains fruitful connections with local vets. He has a lot of experience selling on a one-on-one basis to conventional owner-operated institutions. He practices traditional veterinary medicine and is endowed with a natural talent for sales. When we were a small firm based in the rural Midwest, this strategy served us well. On the other hand, Ed is now in charge of a sales team that has locations all over the nation. Consolidation efforts are now being made in the veterinary sector. Because of this, the majority of our sales are now being made to procurement specialists as opposed to the veterinarians who operate the facility. Additionally, he is in charge of a digital sales operation that seems to function without his presence. Ed does not seem to have the knowledge or abilities necessary to do these tasks in a competent manner.

Does not Accept Personal Responsibility for His or Her Actions

Taking the initiative is plainly essential to effective leadership. That entails having complete control over all aspects of a team's operations and accepting full responsibility for its achievements as well as its setbacks. Poor leaders often look for someone or something else to pin the blame on. For instance, if the group was tasked with delivering one hundred pairs of pants but was unable to do so, incompetent leaders would point the finger onto a lack of available labor or a decrease in productivity rather than admitting that there was a problem with the way they planned their operations.

When one aspires to be a leader, they should realize that being a leader requires them to be ready to face and overcome obstacles in order to achieve the desired goals. It also involves taking responsibility for one's actions when the team does not achieve its goals. People have a negative impression of leaders who try to shift blame or cast fingers at others because they lack credibility.

Lacking Enthusiasm for the Part They Play

There are some individuals who feel they have no business being placed in a position of authority. Even if they make an effort to complete the duties that have been given to them, the performance of their teams may suffer as a result of their lack of enthusiasm and devotion.

For instance, if you work for a company that is led by a boss who is always moaning about the workload or the needed level of production, it is natural for you to feel disheartened about your job. Leaders who are dissatisfied have the potential to negatively impact others they work with. The discontent permeates every member of the team, elevating it to the position of normative behavior. When a leader does not believe in the job that is being done, it is nearly certain that his or her team will behave in the same manner as the leader.

The Definition Of Objectives And The Responsibilities That Go Along With Them

If you want to be an effective leader, you need to have the ability to assign a specific objective to each member of your staff. This purpose has to be clearly articulated and ingrained in the consciousness of each individual worker at the organization.

It is one thing to work without an objective (for example, a miner who digs the rock without knowing why he is doing it), but it is an entirely different thing to have a clear idea of what one is doing and why one is doing it (for example, a miner who digs knowing that his work is contributing to the realization of the most beautiful cathedral in the city): the motivations will be quite different.

When someone asks, "What are you doing? ", that's when the actual difficulty starts. Answers to the question "And why are you doing it?" tend to be evasive and uncertain, such as "I don't know" or "Because they told me to." Demoralizing people is the worst possible outcome of any situation.

It is very necessary for every employee in a firm to have a crystal clear understanding of where their job starts and finishes. When running any kind of company, you must never, ever, at any point in the process, be uncertain about who is accountable.

Everyone should have the feeling that they are accountable for their job, and they should be aware of what they are expected to do, within what amount of time, and at what expense, if any.

You will see the need of constantly maintaining a training and development route for employees, one that consistently motivates workers to better themselves and pursue new objectives as a result of this realization. This may be accomplished in a number of ways, some examples of which include enabling staff to engage in training courses and allowing for job rotations and other forms of internal employment flexibility.

When beginning to work together with a new partner, one of the first things to do is to be clear, to confront him from the outset on his expectations and the goals that are to be reached.

"What do you see your life being like in a few years from now? Which route to personal development do you intend to take?"

Gain an understanding of his perspective, including what he wants, what he expects from you, the working environment, and the tasks that he will be responsible for doing, and so on.

Thankfully, we are not all the same: there are some of us who want a job at any cost, those of us who want to do it step by step, those of us who don't want to take on big responsibility, those of us who wouldn't work an extra hour of overtime even if it was paid in gold... and then there are those of us who aspire to a profession no matter what it takes. In order to provide their employees with the optimal working circumstances, a manager is expected to comprehend the requirements that are expected of them by their coworkers and, if at all feasible, make an effort to fulfill those requirements.

It goes without saying that one must take care not to fall into the opposite pitfall, which consists of being too tolerant and, most importantly, overly friendly with one's partners. This will never result in anything positive.

Try to deliver a one-time acknowledgment that rewards one of your resources if they really deserve it while you are establishing a development path for them and if they are one of your resources.

You are not required to promise a career progression each year, but you may find many other methods (such as business perks, new projects or new responsibilities, training courses...) to move people along in their careers.

We often find ourselves in a position where we have a large number of talented young individuals who, in their early years of employment, put in a lot of effort, and we have a tendency to overload them with tasks that are more significant than their age and level of experience.

This happens simply because they are available and because they have so much enthusiasm to work: the managers take advantage of this, perhaps removing or reducing work to the veterans in the company who are without a doubt less willing and are now devoid of enthusiasm and are only able to complain about having too much work to do.

Young individuals who are capable of doing their jobs well are always welcome, but you need to be cautious because a resource that is used to rapidly expanding its capabilities will, when it reaches a level where it can no longer develop its career, start to get demotivated since it will regard this standstill as a step backwards in its progression.

Bring forward the young people who are talented, but always follow a route that begins with an apprenticeship so that they may progressively fill tasks of responsibility without missing critical phases of their professional development.

How To Get Along With People Who Don't See Things The Same Way

It was like Eddie Haskell all over again.

During our time in high school, we were both employed at the same well-known fast food business together. When he was with grownups, he had impeccable manners. When he was with me, he was forthright, honest, and sometimes arrogant. It looked as if he had an unusual capacity to get under people's skins, and as a result, he didn't have very many friends. He was certain that he was right all the time, and he made it clear that he expected you to acknowledge this.

I will never forget the day when we all got together on a Saturday night to do nothing more than hang around and have a few drinks. We found ourselves in the middle of an argument over religion, and boy, was it a contentious one! It was so unbelievable to me. The worst possible moment to hold a rational discussion about that topic.

After a few more incidents, we began to grow apart. After all, there is only so much one can put up with in the company of someone who is full of themselves, right?

The Most Significant Obstacle to Advancement

I'm going to share three insights with you that will liberate you to make the most of every connection you have with anybody on the face of the planet.

Are you ready?

First and foremost, you need to accept the fact that not everyone will get along with you.

I am aware. In the world of business, one of the most important rules to follow is to treat benefactors with respect at all times. I am aware of it. There is a distinction to be made between treating other people with civility and acting impolitely toward them because that is how you have been treated.

Second, you need to accept the fact that you will not always find common ground with other people.

Couples who have been married for more than one year and have survived the honeymoon phase are aware of this. While you squeeze the toothpaste tube from the centre, your partner may roll up the tube of toothpaste. While you may organize your socks according to color, your partner could simply throw theirs in the drawer. In contrast to her preference for contemporary country music, your musical preferences may include popular songs from the 1970s.

Even if you disagree on a lot of things, the majority of those disagreements aren't serious enough for you to want to kill your spouse.

Third, you're not going to get along with everyone you meet.

That's not a problem. It's possible to respect other people even if you don't really like them. In point of fact, it is possible to despise another person while yet having some measure of regard for them as a fellow human being.

Keeping this in mind, let's investigate the ways in which we might find common ground with those with whom we disagree.

Finding Common Ground With Individuals Who Are In Opposition To You

Here are three methods in which you and your colleagues might overcome the resistance that exists between you and come to an agreement.

1. Do not pass judgment on what she has to say before listening to what she has to say.

This does not imply that discretion should be lit on fire and thrown out the window as a result. What it does suggest, though, is that you should retain an open mind while you are listening. Hold off on making any judgments until she has finished talking. If you dismiss her thoughts as unworthy of consideration before you ever hear them, you won't be able to listen to what she has to say, will you? Then you won't be able to find the treasure that is buried inside it.

2. Show her enough respect to acknowledge that her viewpoint is just as important as yours.

She has the same opinion that you do, which is that she is correct. Both her experiences and her studies have brought her to the conclusions that are uniquely hers. And when you give it some thought, isn't that how you arrived at your own viewpoint in the first place? Let's hash it out. Determine the reasons that she has for thinking the way that she does. Who could say? You might pick some useful information. But even if you don't, the fact that you made an honest effort to listen to what she had to say will make her happy.

3. Identify a point of common ground, and then proceed from that vantage point.

Even the most diametrically opposed ideas may converge at some time. There are certain experiences that are common to all of us. For example, when you have an issue, don't you want to find a solution to it so that you can put it behind you? Don't you want something to take the edge off the agony when it strikes so that you may get on with your life? There is a good chance that the person you are working with does as well. Her method could be different, but it's possible that she's not headed in such a different direction from you as you might think she is.

Put Yourself In The Position Of One Of Your Followers.

You need to be able to persuade the people you lead to work toward your objective if you want to develop into a successful leader. You would want for each and every member of your organization to become involved. There may be instances when you will need to urge someone to continue doing the tasks that you prescribe, even if they do not want to.

If you have ever attempted to lead a group of people in the past, you are aware that the activities outlined above are far simpler to discuss than they are to really do. The failure of many individuals to be good leaders may be attributed to a wide variety of factors. However, one of the causes that comes up time and time again has to do with the gap that exists between the leader and the people who follow him or her.

Your followers are only concerned with achieving their own objectives.

The majority of individuals have the misconception that all they need to do to be good leaders is convey the mission to their followers. However, they discover the hard way that this isn't enough to influence the conduct of other people and that it requires more than that to do so. Learning about other people is the first step you should take if you wish to have an effect on how they behave.

Most individuals are focused entirely on themselves. They have the mentality that they are the main character in their own film. They believe that every other individual is a supporting character who will contribute to the development of their narrative. It is really difficult to shift one's mentality to think differently about this.

Your followers think in a manner that is similar to your own. They never stop thinking about what's best for themselves in the long run. They do not have any interest in the objectives of the organization. The majority of them do not care about the amount of effort you put in as a leader. Instead, they are more concerned with making progress toward the accomplishment of their own individual objectives.

As a leader, it is your responsibility to learn about the objectives that are important to those you lead. You have to find out what it is that they want out of life. It could also be helpful to learn about the things that are most important to them.

You will be able to modify your approach to inspiring others who follow you after you have gained knowledge of these factors.

Learn more about your audience by putting yourself in the shoes of your followers.

The majority of managers are so concentrated on the objectives of their organization or firm that they do not give any consideration to the feelings of the people who follow them. The result of this is that the followers are often dissatisfied, and as a result, they end up neglecting the aims of the firm.

It is normal for dissatisfied workers, for instance, to believe that their firm does not care about them or their well-being in their jobs. People who are lower in an organization's hierarchy often have the misconception that upper management has never done the work they perform.

Employees who are dissatisfied with their jobs sometimes get the impression that they are seen more as resources than as human beings.

The majority of the time, the workers' sentiments are entirely warranted. The people who create policy in most large organizations have never had the experience of toiling away at physical labor for eight hours a day. Because of this, their workers see them as authoritative leaders who deserve to be obeyed. They are not considered to be prominent leaders in any capacity.

The only time that authoritarian leadership is effective is for tasks that are completed quickly. On the other hand, if you want to influence individuals in the long run, you may need to adopt a more strategic strategy. Putting yourself in the position of the people you are leading is the best way to get knowledge about them.

If you want people to follow you and trust what you say, you have to give them the impression that you care about them and their well-being. Try to perceive things from your followers' point of view in order to demonstrate to them more clearly that you understand them and care about them.

You may do this by being more knowledgeable about the minutiae of the lives of some of your followers. For example, during your lunch break, extend an invitation to one of your followers to join you in eating lunch. You might question him or her about his or her personal life while you are both eating. Ask them more questions such as where they live and how they get to work from their residence. You might also inquire about the members of their family. When you do this, you will almost immediately establish a relationship with your followers.

There will be those individuals who are hesitant to open out to you. By revealing aspects of your own private life, you may coerce others into confessing about the inner workings of their own lives. You should be ready with tales that would convey a vulnerable state. If your followers witness you being vulnerable, it may inspire others to do the same.

After lunch, when you are alone yourself, you may give some thought to what it must be like for that individual to go to work every day and carry out the responsibilities assigned to them. In this approach, you will have an understanding of the reasons behind other people's actions.

Is Succesful Completion Of Difficult Tasks Necessary For Leadership?

The majority of us react very negatively when we hear the term "failure." The fact that we despise it to such an extreme degree makes it hard for anybody to consider anything good about the term. On the other hand, it is an open topic as to whether or not someone can ever become a real leader without first experiencing the feeling of having "failed." The first move that a leader often takes that ultimately changes the course of his life is one in which he or she fails. You have, without a doubt, experienced defeat at some time in your life. You must be thinking at this point that there must be some upsides to being a failure on your own. It's possible that this may come across as quite weird to you. Let us take a look at a few more instances and get an understanding of the ways in which failure may assist you improve the objectives you have set for your life and make you a leader.

Illustration A: Imagine that you are a person looking for work who is exerting a great deal of effort to do so, but that all of your efforts are ultimately fruitless. Then you decide to establish a company, but unfortunately, it is not successful in impressing your clients. You find that you are also unsuccessful in other endeavors.

You will have two options available to you if you find yourself in such a predicament: • Defy the odds and attempt to stage a comeback.

or Resign yourself to your fate and continue to be unsuccessful.

In a situation like this, you will need to make some modifications after careful consideration and then make a return to reestablish your reputation. People who have no self-control will eventually give up to their fate, but a real leader would never go that route. He will succeed again after drawing wisdom from his past mistakes.

The quality that distinguishes a genuine leader from a pretender is not infallibility but rather tenacity in the face of adversity. A genuine leader is one who grows as a result of their failures. You are not need to offer the excuse that you are unable to get up again due to your failures, even if you are making a number of mistakes or even a disaster. No matter how many times you have been wounded or how many times you have been unsuccessful, you should always have the confidence to come back with all of your excitement because the possibilities in life never really vanish for those who sincerely aspire to achieve in life.

A regular man will, over the course of his lifetime, experience failure a far greater number of times than a leader will, but the difference between the two is that a guy with a determined attitude will not give up until he achieves success and becomes a true leader. In point of fact, ordinary guys are capable of rising to the position of great international leaders.

The gap between a leader and an ordinary man is so narrow that it cannot even be adequately articulated. A common man is someone who does not give in to the hurt to his heart that the word "failure" inflicts, and a great leader is built out of a common guy who fails over and over again but continues to grow as a result of each of his setbacks. A regular guy who makes every effort to comprehend the rationale behind failure and who never judges others for the mistakes they make is the kind of person who has the capacity to rise to the position of leader.

It is possible for a guy to develop into a leader if he does not like making explanations for his mistakes and does not do it very often. A common guy who is able to assess himself as a failure and comprehend the factors that contributed to that failure is also a man who has the power to develop into a leader in the not too distant future.

Failure and success are not just two words that can be used to describe the nature or characteristics of a common man and a leader; it is neither the qualification nor the distinction between the nature of a common man and a leader. "Failure" and "Success" are not just two terms that can be used to describe the nature or characteristics of a common man and a leader. These are only some of the terms that may be used to determine whether or not an individual have the power and the confidence to confront the whole procedure fearlessly.

Even though you are only a regular guy right now, you still have the potential to become a real leader someday. You have the ability to be the kind of person who is not just interested in achieving success for yourself, but who also really wants to assist others in accurately understanding the potential they have to achieve success in life by courageously confronting their shortcomings. In order for you to attain success, you are going to have to put in a lot of effort. If, on the other hand, you can train your brain to see failure as an opportunity for growth and refuse to follow the herd mentality that says the only way to avoid becoming a total failure is to give up all hope, then you have the potential to become a leader.

If you want to know whether or not you will be the pioneer in that situation, then I must tell you that you will neither be the pioneer in that case nor will you be the last one who will learn a lesson from his own errors. Rather, you will be neither the pioneer in that case nor will you be the last one who will learn a lesson from his own mistakes.

Take Shakespeare as an example; he had to put in a lot of effort to become successful. Shakespeare was a guy who was not only a prolific writer of his time but also a poet and a really inspiring character who never gave up. He was a man who was Shakespeare was a man who was not only a prolific writer of his time but also a poet. He did not come from a wealthy family that might have launched him into immediate success. He came from a home of limited means and became a writer. at the past, he had written plays that were staged at a theater that was situated right next to a bar. Because he still had the charming qualities that people desired, they chose to see his plays over going to the bar in order to do so. He was successful in creating a taste to his plays that people can only discover in his plays and not in the work of any of his competitors. People can find this flavor only in his plays.

Because he never learned how to slow down or stop, he was able to rise to the position of leader despite his humble origins. This was more important than the fact that he was endowed with an endearing personality. He chose to get back up and make a return with some magical charm to generate, and he eventually became the global leader in playwriting.

One further illustration of how a narrative of failure may be turned into a success is shown here. These kinds of tales of triumph are not written in a single day, but rather over the course of many years.

The story focuses on the well-known soccer star Park-Ji-Sung, who hails from South Korea and is most recognized for his time spent playing for the Manchester United club. He was never given any consideration by the soccer teams in his home nation, but he was a successful player for Manchester United, which is consistently ranked as one of the most successful clubs in the world. He might have been a failure simply due to the fact that the coaches of his own nation never paid any attention to him, but instead he proved himself to be a successful leader who played without becoming disappointed to demonstrate his love for soccer. He showed that he had a passion for the sport. He did not succeed in the tryouts for any of the clubs, but he did not give up.

He never tried to make up flimsy explanations for his shortcomings. On the contrary, he used his speed as his primary offensive tool. If he had given credence to the idea that he would fail simply because he was an average guy, he never would have been able to become the first player from his nation to play in the European top division.

Not only did he play for the club, but he also had the opportunity to play for the national team of his native country. In later years, he also rose through the ranks to become the captain of the national soccer team in his home country.

If you want to be a successful leader in any industry or area of work, it is obvious that you do not need to be wealthy or have all of the facilities to work with in order to do so. Being a good leader does not need anything particularly talented on your part, either. Simply by virtue of the psychological distinctions that set you apart from other individuals, you have the potential to hold a leadership position on a global scale. Even in the midst of disappointment, you must train your mind to have the mentality of "never giving up." When you achieve success, it is important to keep in mind that you should never let your ego become too big, since preserving humility is the first step in keeping one's achievement. At the end of the day, these are the most important qualities that a person must possess in order to become a great leader.

Obtain A Reputable Standing

Receiving a communication from someone we despise or do not trust is frustrating for everyone. When I was in high school, I had a classmate who shared my fascination in the idea that different people had different perspectives of the same thing. We came up with a concept that we term the "reverse lie." This is the stage in which you constantly deceive a person until they no longer believe you, at which point you reveal a very significant deception to them. If you ever reveal the truth, it will be the one and only time that they will not believe you.

An easy way to illustrate the concept of the reverse lie is to repeatedly inform a roommate that the liar missed a phone call from his or her parents. When he hears this message, he immediately dials his parents' number, but they always inform him that they haven't called. Eventually, he will learn not to trust you and will begin to believe that you are lying to him if you tell him that his parents have phoned. Therefore, at this point, he will no longer trust what you say. You have a baseline for the reverse lie now that you've established it. Then, his mother phones and says that she has to be picked up from the airport; you give him the message, but he won't trust you, and so she ends up being left behind at the airport.

The intriguing thing about the reverse lie is that even though you're engaging in questionable behavior, you end yourself in a more virtuous position as a result of it. You may say anything along the lines of "I didn't do anything wrong. I have, at long last, been honest with you. I have already informed you that your mother is now at the airport. You made the decision to disbelieve what I said.

This is a really intriguing construct for discussion due to the fact that it is extremely manipulative, and I'm quite sure that this is a notion that the majority of politicians are very acquainted with since it is a method to do something bad while still managing to keep the moral high ground. This is why it is an interesting construct for conversation. It's been years since I've even given the concept of the reverse lie a second consideration, but it's clear that credibility of the messenger is of the utmost importance.

Someone we have a negative opinion of, even if they are telling the truth, is not a reliable source of information for us. The manner in which other people perceive you as a person, including your intellect or personality, your knowledge, and your experience, will all have a role in how they interpret the information they are given. A survey that was published not too long ago revealed that ninety-nine percent of the papers published in peer-reviewed journals and inside medical publications, both of which are respected by the scientific community, did not even apply the scientific process. The technique is riddled with significant inaccuracies.

It was also recently discovered, in another research that I read, that pharmaceutical firms are responsible for the publication of fifty percent of those publications. This is due to the fact that one business controls practically all of those journals, and therefore fraudulent studies can easily be published in them without ever being subjected to peer review.

Despite this, we have an innate faith in them since those individuals have more letters after their name. Even while we know that the majority of the articles in there were either placed there by a huge pharmaceutical business, the scientific process was broken, or the data wasn't peer-reviewed, it would still be difficult for you to overcome that and disbelieve an article. Even though I just shared those three pieces of information with you, if I stated the name of one of those particular journals that we all trust and I showed you an article from one of those journals, you would think that it's right. If I showed you an article from one of those journals. This is the power that comes with having credibility.

In our culture, there is a widespread presumption that all scientists are pillars of honesty, that no scientist would ever lie, and that no physician would ever lie for financial gain. In spite of the mountain of information indicating that physicians and scientists are just as prone to error as everyone else, for some reason we think that attorneys are all pathological liars, whereas we believe that doctors are always telling the truth.

You need to begin with the audience's view of your general knowledge in order to build maximum authority and maximum benefit when you want to influence and convince others. This will allow you to establish maximum benefit and maximum authority. How much do you really understand about this topic? How well-rounded is your knowledge, in general?

The fact that you have more letters following your name is the simplest approach to demonstrate this. Because I have a Master's degree, I could demand that you address me as "Jonathan Green, MA," and I could even add the phrase "with merit," because not only did I obtain a Master's degree, but I also got a level higher than that. In the United States, we say "cum laude" and "summa cum laude," but in England, they say "with merit," and the fact that I have a master's degree in English lends a little bit more credence to what I have to say. People in the United States hold the misconception that those hailing from England are somewhat more intelligent. Because, for some reason, we interpret an English accent as being somewhat more intelligent, having a set of English letters after your name is even more impressive than having a set of American letters after your name. This is the case despite the fact that earning a master's degree in England takes just nine months, whereas in the United States it takes twenty-four months. You now know the true reason I chose to pursue my education in London, yet despite this fact, there is something about the sound of that English university that is more appealing.

The amount of confidence that your audience has in you as a professional is separate from the trust that they have in you with regard to your broad knowledge of the topic. You're a doctor, but how well do you practice medicine? Time is of the essence at this point and may make a significant impact. One of my buddies made an attempt to enter the real estate market while I was in the early stages of my twenties. He had aspirations of becoming a real estate agent, but it is difficult to gain the confidence of someone in their fifties who is about to spend a million dollars on a property. When you are first starting out in your field, it may be challenging to earn people's confidence in your abilities as a professional. Even though you may be correct, it alone is not enough to solve the problem since there are many other factors involved. Because of this, educational institutions encourage the amount of writing and publishing that their faculty members are able to do. The fact that I am a writer, an author, a published author, and on top of all of that, a best-selling author, contributes to the degree of confidence that you have in me as a professional. This confidence comes from the fact that I am an author.

If I can establish a better degree of credibility and get us to a higher level, it will be easier for you to put your faith in what I say. When you start out with a higher level of credibility, it will be easier to convince others of your point of view and win them over to your side of the debate. If you already have a significant degree of reputation and experience, then you can easily win an argument or clinch a transaction in under five minutes. However, if they do not place a lot of stock in your credibility, you will need to provide a more compelling and in-depth case. It's possible to spend two hours on the same transaction and the same discussion.

Above and beyond this, there is the trust that they have in you as a person. Even if you have a lot of experience and are quite informed about the topic at hand, I can't put my faith in you because of some aspects of your character. The majority of high-level investors and successful businesspeople who operate companies and generate a significant amount of money put their faith in their gut feelings. If they already have a negative feeling about someone, it will be quite difficult for that individual to change their mind about their first opinion of them. I have experience from each of these perspectives. I am well aware of how difficult it is to overcome a negative initial impression, since it has happened to me in the past.

For instance, if you go up to someone and stand immediately in front of them while maintaining full eye contact before you say "hello," the first second of their engagement with you may be influenced by anything going on within their head. They may get the impression that you appeared out of nowhere if they are preoccupied with something else and are not paying attention to anything that is in front of them. This will cause them to wonder, "Where did you come from?" In the beginning, they will feel a mixture of fright, astonishment, and shock. It is really difficult to go through this obstacle. You are not to blame for this circumstance; you did not surprise them in any way. They weren't paying attention to what was in front of them. Their eyes were making contact with you, but you were so focused on turning off their gaze that you didn't notice they were looking at you. On the other hand, the very same person, if they were paying attention and observing you, the interaction and attraction would be perfect.

Take into account

Effective leaders recognize that no one has all the answers all the time and so promote issue solving. After some trial and error, I came to the conclusion that explaining the issue at hand, followed by active listening while members of the group participated in a discussion about potential solutions, was the most effective way to arrive at a workable resolution that I had not previously considered. Because team leaders may not always have all the answers, cultivating an atmosphere of thoughtfulness can help the group achieve results that were not initially envisioned. If the team is pushed toward its objectives without being provided with the resources and support that are essential for the team to reach those goals, it will be much more challenging for the team to be successful. Leadership requires many different skills, one of which is the ability to provide resources.

Unwavering stability

Those in leadership roles who are able to maintain consistency accomplish all they do with honesty and fairness. Dependability and dependability are hallmarks of strong leaders. They keep their word and fulfill all of their obligations. At the same time, they set the expectation that every member of the team would see their specific duties through to completion. Self-reflection is a common trait shared by exceptional leaders. They are aware of their fallibility as humans and acknowledge the possibility of making errors. When they do make a mistake, rather of placing blame on others, they take responsibility for it and move on. Great leaders are also aware that the accomplishments of the whole team are directly proportional to their own, and as a result, they take equal credit for the achievements of the group.

A surety or faith

The most exceptional leaders exude self-assurance without coming off as arrogant. They respect the work that is done by all of their subordinates while at the same time providing feedback that is sincere and designed to improve performance. The leader of the group is aware that the group's objectives can be accomplished, even if doing so will be challenging, and he or she conveys this knowledge to the members of the group as an expectation. A leader maintains a constructive outlook, which encourages followers to follow in the leader's footsteps and strive for goals that push the boundaries of the group's capabilities. It is the job of the leader to inspire the members of the team to see beyond their own self-interest and understand that the accomplishment of the team's objectives is in everyone's best interest.

Relationships That Are Successful

There is no such thing as an instant success story when it comes to romance. It will be a long journey, and the process will be gradual and steady. The ability of the two people in a relationship to communicate effectively and to support one another through challenging times is the best indicator of whether or not the two people's connection will stand the test of time.

Couples who have come to the realization that it is possible to be in a happy, healthy relationship are the same couples who have come to the realization that developing excellent communication skills is the key to furthering their link and connection to one other.

Couples who have been married for a number of years have developed a number of communication skills that have helped them effectively comprehend each other. These are abilities that the couple will continue to develop for as long as they are together.

Because you can't ignore issues in a relationship in the same manner that you attempt to avoid your bad feelings, it is vital to communicate in order for the relationship to be successful. You can't just wish it away or act like it doesn't exist in order to make it go away. It is a recipe for catastrophe in a relationship if the partners do not communicate with one another or handle the problems that arise inside the connection, and it won't be long before the connection is severed. The longer you choose to ignore your issues, the more difficult it will be to find solutions to them. It's possible that your spouse wants to speak about and solve these problems, but you don't want to do either of those things. This may lead to a lot of frustration, stress, and resentment over the course of time.

Habits of Effective and Healthy Communication to Implement

The happiest couples did not achieve their state of contentment by some mystical process. They put in a lot of effort to bring their relationship to the point where it is now, and one of the ways that they achieved this was by developing positive routines that helped them enhance the way that they interact with one another. The following are examples of healthy behaviors:

Voicil'appréciation, même pour les choses insignifiantes, et en particulier pour les choses que nous avonstendance à prendre pour acquises. A healthy relationship requires both partners to regularly communicate their admiration and thanks to one another. Thank your significant other or spouse for making you a cup of coffee in the morning even if you didn't specifically ask for it. Say "thank you" to the person who holds the door open for you. It's not necessary to go to great lengths to express gratitude via physical gestures. Throughout the day, sending little expressions of gratitude in the form of notes or texts may make a great impact.

Never Assume: Happy couples always voice their needs and desires to one another. They are good at communicating their wants and needs to one another, which is a skill that every couple should strive to develop. Why not avoid everyone the stress of misunderstanding by asking your spouse directly what they think rather of making the assumption that they will read your mind, catch up on the subtle signs you drop, or know how to predict what you will think next? Assumptions are the source of a significant amount of broken communication, which often leads to conflicts that might have been avoided if better judgment had been used. If there is anything you would want your spouse to do, don't be scared to simply ask them to do it.

Work It Together - If you live with someone else, household duties should be a shared obligation so that no one person feels the pressure of having to maintain the home by themselves. When you divide the workload with a partner, it not only encourages excellent collaboration but also gives you a feeling of satisfaction since you know you can trust on them to participate in the task with you. You should take turns performing the duties so that there is a feeling of justice and balance, and no one person is saddled with the responsibility of doing the same thing over and over again.

Positive Communication: Happy couples have learnt to speak things out, particularly at the phases of the relationship when one or both parties may be going through a difficult period. If you and your spouse take the stance that you will only use positive language while you are having the discussion, it will be much simpler for you to learn how to speak about the things that are tough for you. It lessens the likelihood that things will get more serious and spiral out of control. The use of phrases like "I hear what you're saying and I value what you have to say" or "I know this is difficult to talk about, but I'm here to support you and we can work through this together" are two examples of some great positive language that can be used to help control the conversation and steer it in the right direction.

No Criticism Allowed - When you evaluate your spouse, you make them feel ashamed, uneasy, and sometimes even frightened and tense. This is because you are the one who is doing the judging. Because they don't feel safe enough to open up completely and be themselves when they face this sort of rejection from you, they will lock themselves off to you as a form of self-protection when they go through this experience. It's important to avoid passing judgment on your spouse, especially if it's something you wouldn't do in any other kind of social situation.

Here are some examples of how to maintain limits at home in the form of statements. Learn to recite them.

"The toothbrush should be placed in this container, not the one that's located over there." Show me that you can recall where it should go.

When it is finished, the bowl that is now sitting on the dining table has to be put in the sink. Demonstrate to me that you are able to reach the sink and that you are aware of how to properly put it in the sink. I'm available to work on it with you today."

"When we're frustrated, we don't lash out at other people. Instead, we rely on our own words. Do you really feel the desire to scream? That's not a problem. Let's get it done as a team. I AM IN AN ANGRY MOOD! But please don't hit! "Here, say this, and I'll assist you in finding a solution to the problem. Do it again after me..." "That's okay, and does that make you feel any better?"

When the temperature outdoors is thirty degrees, you must put on your jacket regardless of the circumstances. I know you aren't uncomfortable due of the game you're playing since you're so focused on it. However, you are complaining that your body is chilly, and it is my responsibility to ensure that you do not get ill by failing to keep you warm under any circumstance. I've got your jacket right here. Demonstrate to me that you are capable of putting it on even when you don't want to.

"It's okay if you don't think you can do that correctly; if you think you can't, we can practice it together five times until you get it right." Don't worry about it; I've got all the time in the world, and I'm not going anywhere until you can demonstrate to me that you realize how very essential this is.

"In the same way that I am speaking to you politely, I do expect that you will talk to me respectfully as well. Could you just repeat that? I realize that you are most likely really weary, upset, or stressed out, so please tell me about it. However, please address me in a respectful manner.

"Listen, I would so love to do that art with you again, but the problem is that the last time we did it, all of the water in the cup spilled all over our new carpet, and it made me so sad, and the carpet got dirty. So, it's not really an option." We won't bring out the artwork again until I see evidence that you are able to take care of the mess on your own, okay? We will put it away as soon as you can demonstrate to me that you are capable of maintaining a clean environment in other places for many consecutive days. I have no doubt about that! It will need some practice over the next few days, but after that, I can't wait to use it once again!

Concern, Compassion, And Anticipation

After spending close to an hour in the temple, we emerged with a sense of inner calm and, on the way home, my grandma entertained us with some thought-provoking tales from her youth. On that day, I was given pink clothing as a present, so I knew that my mother would also appreciate the characteristics of the color pink on that day.

After finishing my meal, I went upstairs to seek for the present that had been given to me. I walked into the room and saw a tiny surprise package sitting on the bed, along with a letter that said, "Do you have any PINK color traits? It is time to investigate what lies inside you. Take prompt action." I unwrapped the present, and inside was a stunning pink crystal with the words "Care, Compassion, and Hope" engraved on it.

I pulled out my phone and sent a message to my mother, "Mom, the pink crystal looks more beautiful than any of the other color crystals that you have gifted me so far," and then I sent it. It's possible that the traits represented by all the other stones are ones that should be cultivated for our personal advantage, but the attributes represented by this crystal are the only ones that symbolize being selfless.

My mother gave me a cheery response and remarked, "Good, you are in good form as I expected." And just as the clock on my mobile device chimed nine o'clock in the evening, she sent me an audio message. I made a selection of the message.

CAST OF CHARACTERS INVOLVED IN DECISION-MAKING

People who are able to overcome their fears and make decisions are competent.

Their self-assurance shines through in a trait that observers have described as having "command presence." Regardless of what is transpiring around them, leaders with command presence maintain their composure and do not lose their composure under any circumstances. These people have their lives completely under control. They conduct themselves in a way that is professional and systematic and controlled, with a pace that is appropriate for the circumstance. Comparatively speaking, the pace at which a fireman replaces the battery in a smoke detector and the pace at which they do cardiopulmonary resuscitation (CPR) on a person who is in cardiac arrest are two quite different things.

On the other side of the argument are some individuals who are unable to make a choice that would protect their own life. Indecision may be caused by a variety of factors, including but not limited to ineptitude, fear, a lack of expertise, and a lack of self-confidence. I've borrowed from my own life experiences to construct composite characters (with made-up names), some of whom you may be familiar with. Do you have a connection to any of these individuals?

Be at ease, Chris: Our capacity to complete the work at hand without sacrificing our sense of command is bolstered by our years of experience, professional expertise, superior training, and honed job abilities. These attributes, in turn, have a soothing influence on the people around us; this is what we mean when we talk of command presence. Chris, also known as Calm Chris, is the person that exhibits this trait. An unattended campfire west of Loveland on June 12, 2000 started what became known as the Bobcat Gulch Fire, which was responsible for the destruction of 10,599 acres of grass, brush, and forest. During the course of the fire, there were around five hundred buildings that were under danger. Unfortunately, twenty-two structures and a number of cars were destroyed in the fire. Although I worked as a lieutenant for an engine company, I was not on duty the first day of the fire. The next day, I was informed that I would be involved in the event. In the latter part of that day's afternoon, the fire erupted, resulting in the famous image of a rising column of smoke. Everyone was removed from the fire line and sent to their respective safety zones because of the hazards that were involved.

While we waited for orders and watched the smoke column rise into the air, I kept an ear to our primary radio channel to listen for any instructions. A grass fire was reported in an area known as

Masonville, which is less than five air miles away from where we are now situated. Engine 3 was rushed to the scene. We couldn't help but wonder whether Engine 3 was being dispatched to a brand-new blaze, a spot fire that had broken off from the main body of the Bobcat Gulch Fire, or to assist people who were worried about the Bobcat Gulch Fire.

Calm On Engine 3, Chris had the position of lieutenant. Although he is now retired, he was well-known for his abilities to battle fires and maintain his composure in dangerous situations. Our response came when he radioed the dispatch center and informed them, "Notify the Sheriff that we need to evacuate Masonville." According to his radio transmission, the Bobcat Gulch Fire had spread into an adjacent valley, putting the whole ridgeline that was located to the northwest of that site in danger. The radio report that Chris gave was delivered with such composure that one could have been led to believe that he had just placed an order for a cheeseburger at a fast food restaurant. He had a professional command presence, which is characteristic of those who are able to manage stress well.

Affiliate Leadership

Affiliate leadership, which is closely tied to the laissez-faire leadership style, is one of the leadership philosophies that elicits the most passionate responses from followers. Leaders of affiliated organizations make emotional appeals to their followers in an effort to build and fortify the emotional links they share with their followers. This may be accomplished via the use of positive reinforcement, with the primary emphasis being on creating an environment in which everyone, including leaders and followers, feels supported, respected, and heard (Tobin, 2020). The most important goals for a leader of an affiliate group are to exhibit empathy and tolerance, as well as a dedication to the peaceful settlement of conflicts. Instead of resolving disagreements within the group merely on a professional level, the affiliate leader will make an effort to comprehend the psychological underpinnings of the issue and will work to find a solution on a more individual level. In addition, affiliate leaders use a more flexible approach, which enables their followers to think about other options, work together with other members of the team to discover answers, or ask for assistance from their boss in order to have a more flexible schedule. On the other hand, there are methods of leadership that depend on strict adherence to timetables, regulations, and procedures.

This strategy does have some advantageous side effects. According to Tobin (2020), many leaders have found that this tactic improves the morale of their people by making them feel valued and respected. When they have the sense that their efforts are valued and recognized, followers tend to be happier and more productive in their assigned tasks. When leaders demonstrate that they are paying attention to the issues that are important to their followers, it helps followers feel more confident in both the leader and the organization. As a result, this inspires the people who follow the leader to act in a way that is beneficial not just to the company but also to themselves. Affiliate leadership, much like delegative leadership, takes a hands-off approach to management. This type of leadership aims to create an atmosphere in which followers are encouraged to take the initiative and work autonomously. Affiliate leadership, although advantageous in certain aspects, nevertheless has limitations that encourage originality and innovation in the process of problem-solving. This style of leadership is characterized by the leader's ability to motivate subordinates by invoking pleasant feelings, lavishing praise upon them, and fostering "happy thoughts." Because they care about keeping everyone happy, leaders of affiliate groups try to steer clear of conflict and other stressful circumstances. However, this may cause the leader to lose track of the aims or goals that the group has set for itself. When the perspective of a leader is dismissed or ignored in favor of that of a follower in the process of performance evaluation, this may also lead to conflict. If an affiliate leader spends an inordinate amount of time responding to the emotional needs of their members, the production of the team may suffer as a result. If average performance is considered "good enough" in this aspect, what incentive is there to achieve above and beyond?

Intelligence About Emotions

Being able to recognize and control your own feelings, as well as those of yourself and others, can make you a more effective leader. Steve Gutzler, a well-known thought leader and speaker on leadership, emotional intelligence, and personal transformation, is quoted as saying that "Emotional intelligence can be the game changer to higher performance and personal leadership." In the next chapter, we will discuss what emotional intelligence is, why it is significant, the value of emotional intelligence, the relevance of emotional intelligence for recruiters, and the signs of emotional intelligence.

WHAT EXACTLY IS INTELLIGENCE RELATED TO EMOTIONS?

Emotional intelligence is defined in the following manner by Andrew Coleman in the Dictionary of Psychology: "Emotional intelligence is the capacity to be aware of, control, and express one's emotions and to handle interpersonal relationships, judiciously and empathetically." The terms "proceeding," "using," "understanding," and "managing" emotions are included in the definition of "emotional intelligence." A number of studies have shown that people who are strong in emotional intelligence also have better mental health, are more successful in their jobs, and are better equipped to take leadership roles. It is twice as significant as general intelligence or any technical knowledge since emotions are a component of every human contact, and research indicates that this feature accounts for 67% of all talents that are crucial and required for the performance of outstanding leaders. People were formerly counseled to bury their feelings when they went to work or to keep their emotions out of the decision-making process altogether. This advice was given not too long ago. This perspective was consistent with the mindset that judgments need to be made entirely on the basis of reason and facts. Having said that, this viewpoint is undergoing certain shifts. People who have developed their emotional intelligence are better able to comprehend criticism, understand themselves, and comprehend the perspectives of others. People who have a high emotional intelligence are better able to handle both their talents and their flaws, which ultimately results in better outcomes.

People who are emotionally intelligent often have more equilibrium in their lives and are able to address challenges in a level-headed manner. During a presentation that Caroline Stokes gave in 2017 at the Recruiting Trends and

Talent Tech Conference, she forecasted that emotional intelligence will become an increasingly important talent for workers in the years to come. She gave the example of the United States Air Force, which had just made the transition to recruiters with a higher level of emotional intelligence and as a result saved $3 million in operational expenses.

In a similar vein, the World Economic Forum advises us that cultivating abilities in emotional intelligence should be a primary goal for all businesses since "emotional intelligence sets star performers apart from the rest of the pack."

In addition to that, the investigation does not end there. Multiple studies conducted over the course of the last several decades have arrived at the conclusion that managers and workers who possess a higher level of emotional intelligence are comparatively more productive and have better records of promotion and greater rates of employee retention. Companies that either test for or provide training in the many aspects that contribute to emotional intelligence are likely to enjoy greater levels of success in comparison to those who do not.

There are two main reasons why emotional intelligence is so crucial for recruiters: To begin, emotional intelligence is essential to every aspect of your life since it enables you to cultivate relationships that are founded on trust and communication between one another. Take into consideration the possibility of offering candidates with fresh prospects, discovering and comprehending the candidates' motives, and listening to the applicants' worries. Second, if you are able to cultivate emotional intelligence and notice it in candidates, you are able to provide more value to the business than you would otherwise.

Now let's think about the core qualities that a recruiter needs, and let's place "emotionally intelligent" at the very top of the list. Because of your high level of emotional intelligence, you are able to build connections with candidates that are founded on trust and open dialogue. You will be able to recognize emotional intelligence in other leaders, and new techniques to recruitment will make it clear that developed emotional intelligence is a prerequisite for employment.

Now, let's think at how emotional intelligence may be used in a different way to the recruitment process. The more traditional methods of recruitment are often motivated by cost, and they promote diversity via sourcing. In conventional methods, it is required of recruiters to have an understanding of job preferences, to be able to accept orders and create matches, and to have the capacity to broker relationships. However, let's include emotional intelligence into our strategy for recruitment. What takes place? The new strategy would then be structured as follows: it would be quality driven, and recruiters would have the ability to understand a candidate's career motivation, serve as executive career coaches, be able to consult on role design based on their knowledge of the industry, and drive diversity through the definition of what is needed.

Flip it on its head.

When I was working for a high-tech business as an internal sales trainer, I once went to my coach with a very detailed complaint about the CEO of the company. I went into great detail. I let him know that in my opinion, the other person was completely inefficient and dysfunctional in his role as a leader. I said that working for someone like that was debilitating and like being suffocated. He listened with empathy, but I found it a little unusual that his eyes appeared to be lighting up at the same time as he was listening to what I had to say.

"This is gold," he said. "

By that point, we'd completed a sufficient number of these sessions for him to omit the section when he asks, "Are you open to the possibility that...".

"Gold?" I wanted to know. "What exactly do you see that makes you think this is gold?"

"Opportunity," was the word that he used. "I see a potential answer to the question, 'How can I use this?'"

My coach was aware that I had been developing and presenting seminars not just inside but also outside the organization that I was working for, and he was seeking for fresh content. He told me, "This is what you've been seeking for all along. This is the leadership seminar you have been waiting for."

"What... a workshop on how not to become a leader?"

"Yes," was his response. "Do you think that being aware of that would be beneficial for leaders and managers?"

I understood what he was getting at in an instant. After that, I went home and documented the errors that, in my opinion, my employer was committing. After that, I documented the many methods of being (showing up) that, in my opinion, would be necessary to rectify those errors.

The seminar ended up being a big success for leadership and management teams, and it served as the basis for my book 100 Ways to Motivate Others, which is still doing fairly well in terms of sales today despite the fact that it was published quite some time ago.1 The possibilites and opportunities available

You could be feeling as like you've been punched in the belly after reading Will's statistics regarding the rapid pace of change that is happening in our world. There is a strong temptation to interpret these huge shifts and interruptions as unluckiness falling directly on your shoulders. But of course, you are not the only one who can feel intimidated by the situation. It is quite possible that the individuals who follow your lead (whether you are the leader or the coach), will have a very human and unfavorable response to the changes that are happening in our society today.

When I am coaching individuals who are feeling victimized by the "misfortune" of dealing with something new (such as having to conduct meetings by videoconference instead of in-person), I use the same lines of questioning that were used with me when I was being coached. For example, having to conduct meetings by videoconference instead of in-person. After completely addressing the unease, I steer the discourse into the area of chance and possibilities, and from that point on, the issue may be immediately rerouted into a creative endeavor. This so-called stroke of bad luck is quickly transformed into a potential window of opportunity. This change in perspective is at the heart of what makes successful leadership possible in the modern world.

Proceed with action

Create your own personal meanings for the terms "economics" and "politics." Spend no more than ten to fifteen minutes on this activity at the most. And before you even attempt to write down your own definition, don't even think of consulting a dictionary.

B. The most important ideas. Principles may be thought of as mental models that facilitate increased comprehension on your part. Despite the fact that they do not precisely replicate the actual world (no model ever can), they are nevertheless rather helpful. The more concepts you are able to internalize, the more you will be able to apply those concepts in a variety of settings, and the more information you will be able to learn.

Listed below are some illustrations of different principles:

This is known as the 80/20 rule. Eighty percent of the outcomes you get are a direct consequence of twenty percent of what you do.

Neurons that form connections with one another also fire together. The more you do something, the simpler it becomes because you are either creating new brain connections or strengthening the ones you already have.

When Charlie Munger was in his "believed" mode, he would say things like, "Show me the incentive, and I'll show you the result." The incentives that are offered to people or those that are forced on them have a significant impact on the behaviors that they exhibit. For example, Adam Smith said in his book "An Inquiry into the Nature and Causes of the Wealth of Nations," which was published approximately 250 years ago, that "Workmen... when they are literally paid by the piece, are very apt to overwork themselves, and to ruin their health and constitution in a few years." This was written in reference to the fact that workmen were paid by the piece. An incentive such as this one is an example of one that is counterproductive.

If you have a greater number of mental models at your disposal, you will typically be able to make more informed choices and your learning will be more efficient. When it comes to choosing decisions, the most astute individuals on the face of the earth have hundreds or even thousands of options at their disposal.

C. Laws (the field of physics). In their most fundamental form, laws may be seen as mathematical assertions. Every every time, they have to be correct; otherwise, they wouldn't be laws. That is to say, each and every time we carry out X, we must get Y. The law of gravity is a nice illustration of this point. Every time, an apple will make its way to the ground after falling from a tree. This is a regulation that has no exemptions whatsoever. We never see the situation taking the other turn.

In fields such as mathematics and physics, having a solid grasp of the basic rules is absolutely necessary.

Theoretical Models

Theories are hypotheses that are supported by extensive research and interpretation, as contrast to laws, which are derived from facts and describe how some aspect of the natural world functions. Laws are immutable, while ideas may develop throughout the course of time in response to new evidence.

Here are some instances of different theories:

The hypothesis of the Big Bang

Theories such as quantum field theory, evolution as described by Darwin, Einstein's general theory of relativity, and more

Learning the fundamental concepts that underlie your area of study is a necessary step on the path to becoming more educated.

E. The Most Essential Steps

When it comes to mastering practical skills, the most crucial movements and methods that you will need to master are referred to as fundamental maneuvers.

By seeing the practices of experts in the field, we may get some assurance that basics play an important role. If you take a look at athletes, chess players, or performers who are at the top of their game, you'll find that they always come back to the basics. They make sure that its trunk is as sturdy as possible. Think about those who are skilled in martial arts. They repeatedly put in thousands upon thousands of repetitions of the identical punches and kicks throughout their training.

To summarize, one of the primary reasons for the ineffectiveness of your learning is that you do not spend enough time and effort on strengthening your tree trunk. Instead, you squander too much energy on adding flimsy branches and leaves that are on the verge of falling off. If your trunk is weak, you don't have any strong foundations on which to construct your knowledge, thus you can't grow.

Therefore, you should become an expert in the basic ideas, significant principles, rules, and theories, or fundamental moves that are necessary to thrive at what you do. Don't ever think you already know everything. If you aren't at the top (yet), it's likely that you need to revisit the basics and continue to work on shoring up your foundations.

Dress for Success!

I believe that if you want to be a good leader, you should present yourself in a way that is consistent with that role. People are more likely to react positively to leaders who are clean, well-groomed, and dressed correctly. In his book "How to Get Rich," Donald Trump makes the observation that "the way we dress says a lot about us before we ever say a word." I recommend that you make an investment in clothing of the highest possible quality that you are able to buy. The vast majority of managers do not understand the significance of this idea. Do not misunderstand me; I am not suggesting that you run out and spend a fortune on new clothing and accessories. It is not necessary to wear clothing from a well-known brand in order to have a good appearance. A decent watch can often be purchased for roughly fifty bucks. It won't cost you more than thirty bucks to get a decent pair of khakis. You need to maintain a nice appearance by keeping your fingernails trimmed and your hair cut short. When you walk into a room, people immediately take note of your looks. Simply putting effort into your appearance might make others see you as a more capable leader. It is important that you dress as though you do want to be noticed by other people. Being too flamboyant is never more appealing than displaying elegance. When they are at work, men in leadership roles shouldn't strive to look like rock stars. The women shouldn't try to look as fashionable as the next model to appear on television. At the workplace, you should avoid using an excessive amount of body spray or fragrance. There is a possibility that some individuals are allergic to the odor, while others may feel that it is distracting to their job. You will fare much better if you make an effort to wear just a trace quantity of a quality fragrance.

Using A Combination Of Infusion Points: My Own Personal Experience

It is not necessary to be acting in a formal capacity in order to experiment with nudging infusion points. Every obstacle presents a covert window of opportunity for you to improve your leadership abilities.

My family and I have been in Singapore for the last 12 years, and throughout that time we have had a domestic assistance. Because we had become used to having a helper, we did not give any thought to the chores that needed to be done around the home. She has a history of doing all of her job to a very high standard. She quit our work two years ago citing an unexpected family obligation as the reason. We were in a position where we did not have anybody to assist us for the first time in twelve years. We were unable to find a suitable substitute in a timely manner. The amount of work I had to do kept me quite occupied. My wife Sindu was very occupied with the operation of her company. They were so used to having a helper at home to cook, to wash, to clean, and to retrieve their forgotten toys when our children were 9 and 10 years old during that time.

When we asked our children to assist with the chores, they were reluctant and said, "That is not our job."

At that time, I became aware that I needed to switch to a different tactic in order to be successful. Take a look at the many Infusion centers that I used to get my children involved in the activities listed below. I'm just using this to illustrate a point, but it should be very obvious how you might work anything like this into any kind of conversation.

We sat down with the children and explained to them what was going on in the larger context. At first, I appointed my offspring to the position of head of welfare and security (Prestige). I addressed the child directly and asked, "You really want to guarantee that our home is protected, don't you?" Keep an eye out for anything potentially dangerous and remedy anything that might lead to slips, trips, or falls. Lock all the entryways, turn off the lights, and shut and lock all the windows.

He had a sense of significance and took command of that task. Later on, I would choose him to be in charge of the cleanliness (Prestige) of our family, and he would be responsible for the disposal of garbage.

Then I stated to both my kid and the girl, "We people need to eat in order to live, and that is significant."But the vast majority of people never learn how to prepare their own meals. Assuming that you are able to prepare the meals that you like the most, you are free to go to any region of the globe and continue to consume the kinds of meals that you enjoy the most. You are not going to consume unhealthy food, which will prevent you from becoming weak. You will put away a significant amount of money!" (Prestige, Pleasure,

Productivity, and Profit)... That sparked their attention, which in turn cultivated their competence and stoked their joy for cooking. They started helping out in the kitchen with the intention of picking up useful life skills as a result of their work there.

Cooking, doing laundry, cleaning, and ironing were the many chores that were distributed among the four members of the household, one at a time. In addition to that, I was given the job that nobody else wanted to perform, which was to wash the dishes and clean up the kitchen. Everyone worked diligently with a lot of passion and enthusiasm.At first, it was difficult, but after a week, everything had been put in its proper place. By the end of the second week, we had come to the conclusion that we did not need the assistance of a new person and that we could have avoided spending a significant amount of money early on had we merely been aware of how to access the Infusion points of each person. Even the children picked up new behaviors that increased their degree of independence.

Think about how to present your thoughts in a manner that appeals to different infusion points whenever you are faced with a difficulty that requires you to persuade people to adopt your point of view.

Chapter 9: The Fear of Sharing Knowledge and How It Links Professional Hierarchy in Corporations'A senior–junior' relationship should map as a professional version of a teacher–student relationship (up to a certain degree with correlated variations), and if this relationship persists, then pure professional communication flow will permeate throughout the corporate culture, with sustained realization of continuous learning and growth. The more experienced worker (the student's version) will always learn from the less experienced worker (the teacher's version) how to teach and work together. This indicates that the senior employee and the junior employee work well together, as a growing team, and that this team, being a member of the corporate, would engage directly or indirectly in the expansion of the corporate and the circulation of the leadership culture. But, on the other hand, it has been observed that sometimes senior employees fear "knowledge sharing" with junior employees because they believe that their power and control will be truncated and that they will lose value. However, in reality, they stop learning in this way, which results in them becoming redundant in the long run within the context of proactive corporate culture. In point of fact, more experienced employees should make an effort to improve their capabilities and skill sets by engaging in a continual process of learning, incorporating novel aspects of company control and business sustainability, and passing on his or her prior knowledge base and skill sets to more junior employees (so they may learn). In this method, the senior person maintains their position as the senior person, and the younger person begins to follow the senior person's leadership skills; as a result, the firm grows on a global scale.

From a psychological point of view: Since ancient times, a shadowy feature of human society has been noticed in existence (and the vast majority of us must have heard about it): the teacher strives not to impart every facet of his or her knowledge base to his or her pupils out of fear of losing respect and being subjugated by the student! The instructor has the mistaken assumption that any student would start distancing themselves from their teacher upon the realization that there is nothing further left to learn from the teacher, which would ultimately result in the student disregarding and undervaluing the teacher. This widespread misunderstanding is nourished by "the saturation state" of the instructor, who has no desire to further their understanding. Psychology has shed light on this dreadful but essential fact. When inept instructors or seniors discover that their pupils or juniors are doing better than they are, they experience feelings of insecurity and, as a consequence of physiological mechanisms, the stress hormone cortisol is pumped through their bloodstream. This leads to dread that is mixed with feelings of jealously. However, human psychology also reveals that if a person is continually progressing (intellectually), he or she does not need to fear his or her subordinates (who adore absorbing the expertise and information from his or her senior). But in the event that the senior has not been engaged in an ongoing process of learning and development, the junior would be able to outpace the senior. Sometimes, the senior desires not to learn and develop, intellectually, while at the same time wishing to control the progress of the junior, keeping the juniors in the dark, and thus, sustaining a 'fake respect' culture. In the long term, the corporation stands to lose money if it maintains a work culture like this one, which is characterized by a lack of change.

A LESSON FOR COMPANIES: In order to maintain a good flow of business over time, the "fear factor" of senior employees and experienced workers has to be eradicated, and arrangements need to be established for their continual growth. Additionally, healthy "senior-junior relationship" norms need to be promoted. If this were not the case, the company would not be able to get the maximum amount of productivity out of its workforce.